Veronica's Book

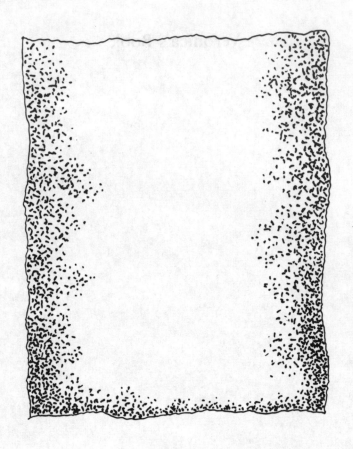

Veronica's Book

Gennady Aygi

With notes on
Sleep-and-Poetry

Translated by Peter France
Illustrations by Igor Vulokh

Polygon
EDINBURGH

© Gennady Aygi 1989
Polygon
22 George Square, Edinburgh

Set in Linotron Sabon
by Koinonia, Bury, and
printed and bound in
Great Britain by
Bell & Bain Ltd, Glasgow

British Library Cataloguing in
Publication Data
Aygi, Gennady
Veronica's Book.
I. Title II. France, Peter, 1935-
891.71'44

ISBN 0 7486 6045 3

The publisher acknowledges
subsidy from the Scottish Arts
Council towards the publica-
tion of this volume.

This English translation of *Veronica's Book* is published
with the authorisation of Le Nouveau Commerce, Paris,
who possess the copyright of the Russian text.

CONTENTS

'He cannot bear to see a cloud upon her face'

Dombey and Son

My daughter is in the country just now. As I write, I can hear her distant voice of some time ago (it is night-time, we are travelling by train, she can't sleep, she is four years old already, and she quietly sings a made-up song to herself: 'The moon is my mummy, I fly up to the sky, and she feeds me').

And it is strange for me now to be speaking not of her, but 'in connection with her'. Strange to be switching to 'authorship' – and in doing so I gradually attune my voice in the first place to readers in that country which gave to humanity, through the love of Dickens, a whole 'daughterly' world.

I always wanted a daughter. 'She, the future she' figured even in my most youthful dreams. I think this is partly due to an unconscious revolt against the 'cult of the son' in the people among whom I grew up; from childhood on I was repelled by *manfulness* (of the Hemingway type for instance) and attracted by an indeterminately 'sacred' *femininity* . . . – perhaps indeed this was how I first became receptive to a kind of 'poetry of nature'.

My generation grew up without fathers. I need only say that in my village there were 300 households and that more than 200 husbands never came back from the war (some of those who did return became the nucleus of the collective farm and village council mafia – I can personally vouch for this – and their violence and cruelty were directed precisely against this poor *femininity*, which still flickered on like a faintly burning candle in the depths of history.

The coming of a daughter was for me, above all, a renewal of womanliness and femininity in my tribe (and this at a time when my tribal roots – as if they still flamed brightly *somewhere* – were burning ever more intensely within me).

Let me put it still more clearly. The birth of a daughter was for me the *return*, the *resurrection* of my mother. My mother, who died early, still appears to me as a kind of *sacred shining* in the midst of a life which has been all but transformed into a 'natural' hell by the dreadful power of the immense Opposite Semblance of the people.

For me the 'people' too is simply my mother and her sufferings. And this *other people* of mine (the real people, not its *opposite*) has in the last analysis only persisted in dreams-as-in-snows ('Ever further into the snows' is the title of my most recent book).

One further point: long ago I began wondering why in the world of art there exist *canonic* forms of mother-hood, whereas *paternal feeling* in literature generally means no more than the 'paternal instinct'.

And in my daughter's 'Book' I tried to give shape to the principle of *fatherhood* (there are in European literature a few works in which 'fatherly' feeling is expressed *post factum*, one of the earliest of them being perhaps the 'Laments' of the sixteenth-century Polish poet Jan Kokha-novski, poems addressed to the memory of his daughter Ursula).

A small group of poems is included in this English-language edition which were not published in the first edition of the 'Book'. They are poems about the 'period

8

of likenesses'. I am convinced (and this is a little 'discovery' of mine) that from the first weeks of life up to about the age of three, children *experience*, undergo and bear, both in and upon themselves, moments, days, and weeks of *likeness* and *likenesses* with a multitude of relations, both living and 'departed'. The little ones (or rather 'some forces' within them) seem to be painfully seeking and – eventually – finding what are to be their own 'permanent' features.

Where people do not respect one another, they may well love children (the 'flowers of life', as Gorky put it). But *respect for children*, conscious respect for them, always demands a particular spiritual-religious standard (and I leave this statement without any explanatory notes).

It was this awareness that I wanted to express in 'Veronica's Book'. Somewhere in these pages one can sense my recollection of one of the points in Swedenborg's teaching about man, who is created 'incomplete and imperfect' so that in the future he may be 'worked on' by That, of Which it is better not to speak (especially in our so rational age).

Observing children of the age of my daughter in her 'Book', I am astonished now that I was able to see so much in Vernonica's first six months of life. But so it was. And now, when there are already half a dozen translations of the 'Book', I once again *thank my daughter for her book, and 'my' book* – the happiest in all my 'creative' life.

July 14 1989 Moscow   Gennady Aygi

Veronica's Book

My daughter's first six months
January – July 1983

DEDICATION

snows shine white
already grown-up read without me
oh you my ahgagaya
(this word is your second in your house)
with the dark of the head now expands
the dark without minds of our poor Earth
this little book and again
snows shine white

14 November 1983

IN PLACE OF A PREFACE

To my daughter

You do not yet speak in *words*. You express yourself – with your face, your smile, your babble, your 'new-born' (as yet unlearnt) movements – and this often reminds me of the state of the poet before beginning to write (many know this quietness which 'contains something', this kind of 'buzz', the still unformed intonation and the special searching power; the gaps in the rhythm and the tense pauses fuller of meaning than any particular 'sense' – in a word, you are a creator, not yet 'speaking out'. . . – and I have tried, as far as possible, to write down from these 'unspoken words' something which is prompted essentially by you.

And this book is deliberately devoted to your 'wordless' (but as I have said, *creative*) period.

Later we shall talk in words (but that will be something different).

You receive gifts. Love. Toys. My love you already know. 'Toys'? By way of toys, I have included in *your* little book some of my *trifles* of long ago.

Sometimes I sing to you (badly). As your paternal grandmothers and grandfathers would have sung to you. Let some of their songs reach you – in a variant by your father (and likewise a version of a Tatar song). I have also included in your book two youthful tales of mine. Could I have imagined then that a quarter of a century later such a daughter would be born to me?

14 July 1983

13

TWO EPIGRAPHS

Veronica, you are necessary . . .

Leonid Lavrov

. . . And
Veronica's Hair, even here – I plaited,
unplaited,
I plait, unplait,
I plait.

Paul Celan

14

PROLOGUE:
CHANT — FATHERHOODLAND

> If we break this oath, may hops sink
> in the Volga and iron float up
> (from a treaty between the Bulgars
> and the Russians, 985 AD)

if
for you I have passed on
then hops will sink
in-love-like-a-sea
(*ay-iya-yur*)
but when *without me you pass by*
iron will float up
from-singing-like-a-sea
(*ay-iya-yur*)

1983-4 Moscow-Kaunas

ON THE DAY OF FIRST MEETING

cloud of veneration
this my slowed-down
looking . . . – and what self-recognition
of another world
circles – close by? . . . – not a look – but untouched
      Word-Face:
oh brief equality: One – it cannot be said! for the same
      Looks
with the same silence
(One – as the face – at the One)

18 January 1983

MY DAUGHTER'S FIRST WEEK

the quietness
where the child is – seems uneven
within limits – of fragile lightshadows: emptiness! – for
    the world grows
in her – to Listen
to Itself
in its Fullness

22 January 1983

HEAVEN-GRAMOPHONE

from the fields
continuing out of pain
soon my child
there will be
for you too a schubert:
Always-Unfinished
above pain
to be unending
from the fields

1983, February

OR — WHO LOVES TO ME

with what then do I love?
or - who loves to me?
I do not know
for – despite all my *obscenity*
so often
for the baby now
I seem – without changing – sacredly-painfully
(it turns in a circle)
pure

4 March 1983

APPEARANCE IN A SMILE

and a flower opened – to smile on the face:
made new
(so much in solitude)
the *mother-come-again*
shuddered:
oh this circle! turn me so: not to come to
     my senses or to visions:
praise to Pity
as to God – for this strange-and-only time:
it narrowed – and flashed past!
I know no beginning or end:
only lightwhirl!
(and so strangely including – me)

4 March 1983

ON DAYS OF ILLNESS

1

the baby's illness the trees' disquiet

2

in velvet of flowers I go to sleep tossing and turning
with cheeks tossing and turning
amid floods: like a dream made of clumsy circles:
of belatedly-needless tears:
as if for my mother . . . or for whom then?
clearly – all the more in this mish-mash – clearly:
in any case – not for our Lord

3

and trees were once
like brothers in mist – into their poverty
Came God amid snowdrifts (Continuing
my silence as work:
with sorrow – amid the trees)

4

oh God the child's shudder

11-12 March 1983

BEGINNING OF THE 'THE PERIOD OF LIKENESSES'

and the forces
of the tribe are stirred – and they float
and turn like wind-and-light – carrying over your face
cloud after cloud: all expressions
of vanished faces –

to manifest to confirm – the 'definitive'
appearance – your own:

with fire – standing firm in turbulence! –

(is it not with this same heat that – peering – I shudder:

as if – amid some singing? –

pain – came in like the wind)

March 1983

AND: NOT TOUCHING

one should fear
both children's fingers and tender
leaves – of birdcherry:

because:

there is nothing and no-one terrible in the world only
    God (stronger than kindness! and remembering –
    keep quiet):

and only:

you know – you

22 April 1983

CONTINUATION OF THE 'PERIOD OF LIKENESSES'

a passing gleam: a shade? maternal?
from what depths: from unspeaking
time – forgotten treasure? dream and not dream:
light – reaching the face: revelation
of whom then deep down
with the flash of a bond – that perhaps also raises
white and dark of ancient field and wind?
or is it grief – flickering – in the little face
of father-wandering through unknown first-circle
in attempts to find himself again
in the rising storm of the tribe?
you sleep. . .– but it wakes – ever wider ever stronger –
    the common-shining:
hammered out in pain
where then is it hiding – your
fresh-and-new-found
appearance – among many others?

April 1983

TRANQUILLITY OF A VOWEL

a

21 February 1982

NOW

to O. P.

my friend
oh   mother-child
            the baby's face moves away
            to have strength
            to come closer shining-quiet
            to the circle-features
            of the loved-and-loving
            (many
            separately
            One)

            2 April 1983

it gleams – without age – the soul of humanity: purified – by the heart of a child (by 'work' – she too works! – or rather: by work – unknown – on her behalf) – revealed to the light – invisibly – 'comprehensible': oh-what-can-I-say! – to such a source: its name is 'it-only-remains unique'! – but what then – just now – is happening? – I look – I forget – I look . . . – forgetting looking

April 1983

QUIETNESS

oh my quiet god
repeating you like a senselikeness
I seem
long since
in a steady calm: cool you flow
without change . . . – only once I glanced round:
the cherries
had already gone over . . . – the child
prolongs the smile . . . – only such gurgles of yours
including old heart's weakness ever more intimate
(with a certain whisper)
from time to time – barely – show forth
the clarity of the treasure 'my quiet god'

April 1983

BED TIME

in my back I feel always
a heaviness 'you have gone'
you drop off (and I start to doze
like some kind of sorrowful
'part')

May 1983

URSHULYA AND THE WILD ROSE

to the two-year-old
daughter of my friend,
the Lithuanian poet
Sigitas Geda

the wild rose bush
is scarlet and broad – and this
she can almost hear
creasing her little brow:
suddenly – alerted – it seems
a jolt of the heart
surprised her:
it trembles – in the little face
it continues to spread:
the look
like the brief halt
of a little cloud

May 1983

A LOST PAGE
(OR: SNOW IN THE GARDEN)

1

a page on the wind

2

bwol bzilda grad
ei tselestine
bzilda and grad
ohei verty

3

and not to be found

1961

IN THE FOURTH MONTH: ATTEMPTS AT SINGING

the most fragile
is the purest: out of
deep light (plain in presence
rather than naming)
showing forth with clear-simple-shining: this miraculous
painfully innocent (just slightly painfully questioning)
a-a-of-lullaby
(in firstguessing
like firstcreation)

12 May 1983
village of Demidovo, Kalinin District

SONG FROM THE DAYS OF YOUR FOREFATHERS
(variation on the theme of a Chuvash folk-song)

> . . . to drink not from a glass, but from a clear spring.
> (Bela Bartok, Cantata Profana)

I wandered through the field and there was
not a single haycock in it

I went into the village
and there I saw
not a soul

and the girls were sitting
behind washed panes of narrow windows
and knotting the lace
full of eyes

I looked in the window and I saw
they were betrothing my beloved
in a white dress they decked her
placed a beaker in her hand
as she stood before the table

– I wept and I rocked
outside your window
and you were quiet –

like a candle on the sill
of a lofty church

'I see' I said silently
I said silently 'farewell'

having no family I understood – 'people'
long afterwards
'there was something' I knew

and I kept nothing in my head
weeping with my cheeks
in my hands

1957-1959

AND: AT FIVE MONTHS

by Breast
or by Heel
(oh how humanly
we figure You)
in power – Entering the child
in the face – in miniature – Taking Shape
You Gaze – Seen by us: and I seem in the wind
tremblingly enfolded – scarlet

6 June 1983

SONG OF THE TATAR GIRL

I took a bucket and I went for water
because there was no water at home.
I sat down beside the bucket and wept
because there was no happiness.

And in those days I was hardly
taller than the bucket.

'Mother' I whispered – the clearing fell silent,
'brother' I said – the dream grew quiet.
What I called by name was silence:
the sun, the oaks, the wormwood.

And to my song alone,
outside the village,
I secretly sobbed out – 'sister'.

1958

TEA ROSE — THE ONLY ONE IN THE NEIGHBOURHOOD

in the face
something added — as if by the wind:
seconds of trembling in it
seem the body — of calixity:
in the temples — seems the weight of folds
rounded and gentle: with sorrow

26 June 1983
Chernomorka, Odessa

NOTE — AFTER ROCKING

to J. S. B.

She painfully looks for a *pacifying rhythm* seeks a *near-melody* from herself and I all unawares *in order to help her* begin to hum a cradle song of my own invention to that melody whose *outlines* were just now tormenting her and she goes to sleep I have noticed several times that her *attempts* at singing to herself and her *fragments* are like the birth of *something* (like a child's little steps) I would say 'for bach' oh what a heart he must have had the father – with such a compassionate maternal spirituality – of the lullaby *spheres*

27 June 1983
Chernomorka, Odessa

STORY OF THE LEVEL-CROSSING GATE AND THE CROSSING KEEPER'S CABIN

A striped old Crossing Gate
was quite sure of being
the Track's one and only suitor.
And boldly thus he spoke:
'My dear Railway Track,
for the last twenty years
I have been bowing to you,
isn't it time you took notice?'
But the Railway Track answered:
'My dear Crossing Gate,
you are only acquainted
with one small part of me,
you don't know all of me.
I have dozens of admirers.
You had better look for someone
who can be seen at a glance.'
Only the Crossing Keeper's Cabin
overheard this conversation.
She stood opposite and wept:
'Lord help me, like a fool
I thought it was to me
he was bowing all these years.
Oh why
did I not die
before this day!'

1958

PURER THAN A TEAR

purer than a tear
this dribble: innocent life
shines in it! – joy:
out of purity
of substance
expressed:
oh Lord
to me

June 1983

ROSES OF ETERI AGED THREE

angels

read
your book

and when were the pages opened?

they sink
(and the mind
any moment
will take flight)

oh windlikeness

swoon
(greater than me)
consumed

1983

RECOGNITION OF THE NAME

whirl of feelings perhaps
(like vertigo)
before consciousness
(as before a mirror) :
with some power of sight gleams
and disappears
like some imprisoned shade
the shy – with quiet pauses
babble
of something

June 1983

STORY OF HARLEQUIN GROWN OLD

When I strolled down the streets,
chessplayers crowded in my wake
and mentally worked out their moves
on my breeches.

And when I came to the theatre,
all the dolls stared at Harlequin,
and carefully concealed the threads
that pulled at their arms and legs.

And when I put my hands behind my back,
they were like white bunches of flowers
lying on a blue carpet,
and the Columbines gasped after me from the balcony
when I went away home.

And when I had worn out my breeches,
the Columbines said that my hands
were like thistles in the open field.
And the dolls all got married.

And now in the deserted castle
I sit on an old sofa with Rex the yard dog,
we drink coffee, curse Siamese cats
and this old old story,
there is no way we can end it.

20 October 1958
Village of Krasnaya Pakhra outside Moscow, dacha of
V. R.

43

SMILE (MEANING 'BELOVED')

and he
(the smile and voice)
is the same – but nearby is noise and movement
    (chestnut trees and roses)
and the loved voice
the face
are now just one among others: nearest tree
    among trees
(and yet
that tree: is like the continuation
of the babble
the cries
and the little eyes-wa)

25 June 1983
Richelieu Square, Odessa

44

MOUSE GONE

there she is

18 November 1982

AGAIN: ROCKING YOU

scarlet
roses – touch the eyes
of the baby:
day – be a circle: – oh butterfly:
come in – to mark:
the moment:
with white

June 1983
Odessa

TOPS OF THE BIRCHES — FROM CHILDHOOD AND TILL NOW

as if
still the same:

oh
stillness anew – after
whisper
look
and hearing –

(and I was forgetting this was all my life forgetting the
lullaby that was a voice to remember all my life the lullaby
as if noiselesly-pristine with spirit opening me from the
beginning promising me expansion free without limit) –

oh
stillness anew – (for a long time no-one):

air – in the tops

of the birches

June 1983

AGAIN – SOMETHING FROM THE 'PERIOD OF LIKENESSES'

'oh – you my you'
I whisper-as-I-swing-you
'oh – you the most the most'

not speaking your name! –

and – like a wordless answer – the sleeping child's
    expression
(the wind – through all the face)
steady even when flickering:

seems as if deep down grows ever stronger in some
    way a most-ancient-maternal

secret tranquillity:

like a star
softened – by distance

July 1983

SONG OF SOUNDS

o (a Certain Sun)
in *a*-Heaven (also a Certain one)
to *ye-i-oo-y*-Other (Worlds)
and *a-ye-oo*-Others
to trees-*yu* to insects-*ye* to *a*-children

6 July 1983

IN DAYS OF ILLNESS — DREAM IMAGE

bitter
and damp
was the oneness:
the mouth – having touched the rose
and all
this – transformed into a tear
(dimly
as if
a heavy fault
ancient
in memory):
was I – for a moment entirely
forgetting myself in this
in dessicating – daytime – terror

July 1983

CHUVASH SONG FOR A GIRL YOUR AGE

to a little Hungarian girl, Agi Abel

Ay, the game, the turning game! –
and the high point of that turning
is the spreading elm-tree top,
the top of the elm tree shakes,
drops us into fire and water!

and between fire and water
I brewed beer like fire,
gathered guests, as hair is gathered,
made them play like dolls,
then scattered them like chickens:

– Line up, line up, tsip-tsip

now scatter!

1983

Now
as a little girl
as my daughter.
Like the shining
of my tribe – through the face
in the name of all – in a tear
through the ages undimmed
by emotion (as on the holy face)
now in this day of mine
with you
without words – with you.

1983

LONG WALK

day's
Shining
at full height
(Elevation
in the figure
of Air)
in the harsh wounds
(in air)
of roses

July 1983
Chernomorka, Odessa

AND: SOMEWHERE A LITTLE BOY IS SLEEPING

                                    to a little Serbian boy of your age,
                                              Mita Badnyarevich

this
unseen fire – guarded
by unseen winds
and the house full of people
is ever more wind – when – in a little understanding
we seem ever closer
to that source of light: the strongest – through most
        delicate
weakness: oh as if for the earth – among plants – in
        radiant maturation
it expands – in distant hiddenness
its circle (and all this in the house)
this warmth
that is warmer than earth's possibilities
(unseen – wafted in)

1983

VISION : A YOUNG GIRL

to fling up
in lightning the lines
of delicate temples
and to light up
the eyes with such grief 'in my life
I shall not see with earthly eyes
the most possibly-Beloved
of Your beauty!'
and to leave a memory of the one without whom
perhaps
it will be
more sad
precisely – in happiness (and the whisper
will come: I wish:
here without order scattered
by movements
friend
to you from yourself)

3 July 1983
Odessa

PHLOXES IN TOWN

as if
in the impersonal thinking of the world
quiet and clear
here – as in the centre of a clearing – p u r i t y
                              t r e m b l e s – and we pass by
not disturbing it
even with the imperceptible
breeze of attention

13 July 1983

LULLABY? IT IS YOURS

are you
big or *little?* you
with your whole self – transforming
my heart into a *lullaby* (the days
go by for us
like years) oh more:
you are creating (oh child) with a *lullaby*
my very self: it has gripped me – and the resonance
expands – as if from the kernel
of the utterly familiar! and turns in a circle
    – from the depths
of little-immense
you

19 July 1983

a divine metronome
phosphorescent
Wild Apple Tree
of Childhood's name

July 1983

SOMETHING — AGAIN ABOUT A BOY
(verse for a photograph)

of suffering and pain
of a single kind:
has it happened
in these eyes
the tilt – so clear –

downwards – to the heart? –

as if to mourn
the heart's loneliness –

all – his life

1974-1983

YOUR FIRST SEA WITH ME

1

Moon Submitting to Sea's Concentration Seeking through
Calm Power of Embracing Equalising by Tranquil
Forging

2

    dream
    like a baby's little steps
    in half-darkness
    in noise – heard through sleep – as with
      a baby's body
    for a long time
    little steps

3

Sun Possessing Sea Openly with Paternality of Rays of
Chastity Continuing the Embrace Hammering with
Magnificence

July 1983
Chernomorka, Odessa

AGAIN – TRYING TO CATCH EXPRESSIONS

can one
discern
in the wind – shades of wind? –

again
into a circle of light
circling (as with some question
perhaps: a little – with light) –

as in whispering almost without breathing
and in terror – before the meaning
of the movement of lips –

afterwards – and unconscious! –

I enter-as-I-stray

1983

LITTLE SONG FOR YOU – ABOUT YOUR FATHER

> My father was like a white spice-cake
> (from a Mari folk-song)

My father
was like a white spice-cake,
his goodness
shone white, –

being swallowed
by the air of the day.

And now in that air
there is no-one,
the bedchamber – in winter – becomes an empty
    field, –

being swallowed
by the dark of the day.

And before dawn I dream
of my father's sledge in the field
white as a spice-cake,
a spice-cake,
only there is no-one in it,

but over it
shines and floats
the same – white – goodness, –

being swallowed
by my grief.

1983

WRITTEN DOWN WHILE SITTING WITH YOU ON THE BALCONY

your speech without words! it seems like my intonations:
tunes without words . . . – but what shyness – is yours –
in the content . . . – have I ever achieved such simplicity
of radiance – of enchantment-with-everything! – with a
modesty – that seems to gleam! . . . – with the idea
itself . . . – of innocence

12 July 1983

PAUSE IN MY DAUGHTER'S 'BOOK'

suddenly
(you are sleeping now
but I see
a look)
I must grieve and abide alone:

as if – all dried up! –

:

I lived on and off (broken branch of needlessness
in one thing then another!
at times needful a little in something
but then
nothing
to anyone –

and at times I shuddered – I shrank with compasssion:

in the steady
long-familiar
stillness!) –

:

and you were purest
tear
in the world:
(oh at times to speak with such a tear . . .) –

you were – as in silence
the place – of answer
simple – in simplicity of goodness! . . –

:

and I
(as if in the world
a being
without substance
so strangely
alone) –

longed – to commune in you as in a tear

with your purity

1983

OFTEN FIVE-YEAR OLD ASYA COMES TO SEE US

in Asya
there is overflowing
goodness! and her face knows no limits:
like a noisily-glittering street
over a gully – with a skip-and-a-leap
onward – to shine! and the shining little girl
comes – into our world (yours and mine)
with a smile – still more – outlining
as a guest! . . . and her hands are like a peasant girl's
covered in cuts and scratches 'mummy
lets me peel the cucumbers'
and in the company of these delicate – 'working' cuts
    and scrapes
you and I are as if in the circle
of ancient – poor-most-generous childhood
(encompassing
the infinite world)

July 1983

FIELD DREAM

The Bobolink – the Ocean
(Emily Dickinson)

oh lightest
of winds – from the little
star-face
just perceptible over the frock –

it opens wide for me a special field: to live and have
    our being
with that trueness only! . . . . . the sun
sinks . . . and there among swifts over daisies
is my Bobolink! . . . – on love this sweetest of wounds
is all – your purity:

breath – of the world

July 1983
Moscow, field near Orekhovo-Borisovo

67

CONTINUATION

I must
plunge deeper
into that shining
(not remembering what you are)
and the understanding
shines shines – and this is for another
I – to understand (continuing the shining
in a new forgetting
to others)

1983

PLAYING FINGER GAMES

> And the little finger said: 'But I'll run away without saying anything!'
> (from the words of a children's finger game)

A call, – oh what sudden – with pain – concentration of music – fathomless and higher than any possible 'height': sounds – pre-words! . . . – smile, little teeth – fresher than petals: in whiteness! – tiny nail, questioning look: the world is like a silent question in reply! – again tiny nail, tear, this thin lock of hair on the neck, and the finger: to be entrusted – as a charm – to an angel only – and even then: only in reflection! – babble and nail! . . . – yes, all this equality: before the one measure – veneration.

13 July 1983

AND – OATS IN FLOWER BEYOND THE MEADOW

> Finishing this book, to you
> – out of my childhood

oh dream
the soul is that dream
she is always there in scratches:
the common dream
passes over into a feast-day
and the distance that remains (singing without people)
through and through
rustling
ever more into the distance
is flowering

July 1983

SINGING AND SILENCE

and the little girl-flute sings
when the silence
in the dull-calm city is pure and free
like some field – and also like an echo: brief and fragile
sphere (already she rang out glassily)
in pure concentration
seeming
like a child of god

1983

AGAIN: THE THIRD GRASSHOPPER
(NOW – FOR YOU)

with squeak-and-leap! – sketch after sketch
(drawing – on air) –

with a winglet – he rubs out
with a noselet – puts in shadows

and a wash – of radiance-clearing! signs
with sunbeam-chirrup:

– *here* for me
just a flicker – *everywhere!* –

with his legs? both up and down!
his canvas – just one thing:

the sky – not ever drying! –

he's simply (let me tell you) – old father:

Cha-gall!

July 1983

TO A FRIEND — INSTEAD OF A LETTER

to M. F.

and yet
Friend
when
everything falsely-adult-clearsighted has long
been gathering — in a blind fog
out of the darkness cutting — as if building a world
that is always the same separate-and-from-nowhere
they gaze — flowers and children
(and what besides? — in the depths of hushed pre-vision
ever more ancient and distant
are the cries
the reminders
of the birds)

31 May 1984
Moscow, in the metro

FIRST WORDS

Just half-a-dozen of them: like pebbles in the palm . . . –
taking care – not to drop them – and the awkward
inspection – with a kind of shyness: as if – saying slowly:
'there . . . ' – even a request and a call are modest gifts: of
the whole being.

1983

VISION: YOUNG GIRL

not from me
from another
calling forth – a masterpiece of Poetry
Immortality passed
through the city – and now here contemporaneity
is no more – and the Word
fuses with the Sun
and with souls
in another world – and through it all
gleams
like a gift
her young walk! . . . . . – in an unknown principle
is the best – of her now finished
shining – and of the long
(like fires
burning)
fathers

1983

AGAIN — SHE SLEEPS

again
disturbing with special
quietness
(as if of the spirit) . . . . . . and dear to me
like a wound . . . . . . I bend down . . . . . . and she
    glows
with a criss-crossing
of Bending – as of the Mother . . . . . . breathing
  threefoldness
of pain . . . . . . that aerial Bending
faintly
touching me
with its radiance

July 1983

ABOUT THIS

whether little or much
the gift – of love
will later come to seem
such emptiness it will have to be filled
with great pain: perhaps you will not see it yourself –

(others will see it) –

as with plenitude – achieved by you
it will start to circle! – the oneness
of the silent friend's former gift
and of sorrowful memory:

a modest (like a spot when eyes are closed)
simple human star –

for the world (or perhaps – just for sky and air)

7 July 1984
Dovainonis, Lithuania (raspberry canes in the forest)

SOMETHING PRECIOUS

Suddenly: a glance through the window – and I see just
this: your little hand – among flowers

July 1983

AND : THE FIRST HALF YEAR

you are a *peasant baby* out of Rembrandt
these little feet made to walk on plank floors
to fall (mother cannot see everything)
and the knees are bent – obedient to a simple song (to
    jump and skip – more than to be grateful! to help
    and to sympathise)
the little hands – as if taking bread
(even so – *love* is embraced)
and the kitten-rival 'put in its place' by your
      growing up
in front of the bowl sits quiet
and the Protector? in this picture
he is always in half darkness
with the work (for child and God) of his hands

14 July 1983

EPILOGUE:
LULLABY-SUVALKIYA

it has set
(*kupolya kupoleli*):

the sweet sun – *lelyumay*:

alelyum kaleda! –

(quietly: here comes into
the singing – *Demyadis*:

the Tree of God) –

kupolya kupoleli! –

she sleeps – in her cot
my daughter – *lelyumay!* –

alelyum kaleda

14 July 1984
Suvalkiya, Southern Lithuania

80

&

(September 1983   July 1984)

81

AUTHOR'S POSTSCRIPT

My daughter Veronica (my sixth child) was born on January 14 1983. The poems in this little book were written for the most part during my hours of direct contact with my daughter: when I was taking her for walks, rocking her in the pram and so on. Hence the 'miniature' quality of several of the poems and the 'notational' or observational form of some of them.

21 August 1983

SLEEP-AND-POETRY

(notes)

1

December, – and whenever we are awake – by day or by night – there is always the darkness of December outside the window.

Life is the enduring of this darkness

Such darkness expands space, as if including it in itself – and it is itself infinite. It is more than city and night – you are surrounded by some single limitless Foul-Weather-Land.

You must endure a few more hours of solitary work. You are one of the *sentinels of night* – 'someone must stay awake, someone must be a sentinel', says Kafka.

But you remember the possibility of Refuge, of Salvation even, from the anguish inspired by the Foul-Weather-Land.

And at last you pull the blanket over your head and wrap the other end of it under your feet. And then you wait for Sleep to envelop you on all sides. To fold you into its Lap. You hardly think about what this resembles . . . Some kind of return? To what? To where?

2

A huge headline in *Literaturnaya Gazeta*: 'The riddle of Morpheus solved?'

Perhaps we shall soon be reading: 'The riddle of

waking solved?'

Why is a person composed of waking only, why is he or she nothing but waking, and sleep not merely the person, but something else, something 'other'?

Why are we like strangers to ourselves when we have 'business' with sleep?

Clearly we cannot forgive *sleep* the oblivion, the 'loss' of our 'I' – the very thing that at the same time we so thirst after.

It is as if we were 'playing at Death' with it, without knowing the essential thing about death, just as children play at war, knowing nothing of *murder*.

3

But remember, before the inward sleep merges with the outer – with Foul-Weather-Sleep, – before you become – remembering and not-remembering yourself – existent and as if 'not-born' – remember 'those who are on the march'.

And remember, shuddering, Nerval: in the freezing cold, the empty street . . . – Nerval knocking at the doss-house door. Not recalling, not remembering – his mother . . .

4

Sleep-Haven. Sleep-Escape-from-Waking.

Speaking of the links between Poet and Public, Poet and Reader, we shall consider here only the most recent times, and specific places.

And using the subject before us, let us ask ourselves where, in which writing, there is most *sleep*.

There is a great deal of it in 'non-committed' poetry.

Waking is so much 'everything' that it has not been given a separate God, as sleep has.

But in any case aren't we talking of different ways of looking at one and the same boundless Sea – the conceivably-and-boundlessly Existing.

There are periods – extremely brief ones – when the *truth of the poet* and the *truth of the public* coincide. They are the times of poetry's public action. The audience experiences the same thing that the poet proclaims from the platform or stage. And then we hear a Mayakovsky.

Public truth is the truth of action. The audience wants action, the poet calls to action. Is there any room here for *sleep*? There is no *sleep* in the poetry of the Futurists (only dreams, mostly ominous ones).

8

Sleep-Love-of-Self.

'Innocent' sleep, it seems, is possible on a desert island. However we know that Robinson Crusoe on his island soon found for himself obligations to other *living creatures*. And let us not forget his prayers to the Creator.

9

Poetry has no *ebb* and *flow*. It *is*, it *abides*. Even if you take away its 'social' efficacy, you cannot take away its living, human fullness, profundity, autonomy. After all, it can visibly penetrate also into those spheres where sleep is so active. To 'dare' to dwell in sleep, to draw nourishment from it, to communicate with it, such, if you like, is the unhurried confidence of poetry in itself – it does not need to be shown the way, to be authorised, to be controlled (so too, correspondingly, the reader).

Does poetry lose something in such circumstances, or does it gain? Let me leave this as an unanswered question. The main thing is that it *survives*. Drive it out of the door, it comes back through the window.

10

Waking up is a thousand-fold 'new birth'.

And yet, whence comes this *regret for something* on waking?

Perhaps we are grieving unconsciously for the 'material' of life, which has been consumed, unbeknown to us, during the night – and for the thousandth time – on the dark, wordless bonfire of Sleep?

11

And so the truth of poetry gradually disappears from public places – it retreats into the separate lives of separate individuals.

The reader changes, – now he is not occupied with faceless 'common affairs', now he experiences his life in the light of the problematic phenomenon of Existence. This must not be thought of as his own selfish 'affair' – his experience of existence can be *exemplary,* can show the way – a model of human life. This reader needs a poet who speaks *only for him, only with him*. The poet in such a case is the only companion he can trust.

The 'shape' of the connection between poet and reader is changing. Now it is not from *stage* to *auditorium,* to the *ear*, but from *paper* (often not even from print) to *person*, to the *eye*. The reader is not *led*, not *summoned*; he is *conversed with* as an equal.

12

The general state of sleep, its 'non-visual' atmosphere, is sometimes more important and leaves a greater impression than the dream itself. (As if the atmosphere of a cinema were to affect us more than the film).

I shall never forget an uncomplicated dream I had some twenty years ago: the sun is setting; in a kitchen garden, just above ground level, the leaves of a sunflower are gleaming. I have rarely felt such emotion, such happiness as then, on 'seeing' this dream.

I need no 'Freudian interpretations' here. I simply don't want any ('leave me in peace').

'Symbols'? – You can discover them easily enough.

But you cannot include in the luminous circle of this dream-sleep the most important *factors* (you can only *take account* of them, but you cannot *experience* them, for they belong to someone else): I was sleeping in my native porch, in my native village (and beyond stretched, like a Sea of Happiness, the boundless Field!), my mother was somewhere close by (perhaps in the same kitchen garden . . . perhaps her sleeves were damp from brushing the *hem* of the Guardian-Forest), there was such a triumphant 'presence of all and of each'!* – and the *absent* was still hiding – as from daylight – like a thief in the forest ..

Sleep-World. Sleep-maybe-Universe . . . Not only with its Milky Way, but with a little star too on the outskirts of your village, a star which is perhaps visible to the vision-soul.

13

I hope it won't seem that I consider an increased 'incidence' of sleep the main characteristic of the type of poetry I am speaking of. It has many other aims and many other 'materials' – that is why it is 'non-committed' (we shouldn't expect it to 'commit' itself to sleep after all!).

But since we are talking about sleep, then let us say that the connections of this kind of poetry with the Reader are so intimate that they can *share sleep* with one another.

*An expression from the author's poems

Sleep-Poetry. Sleep-Conversation-with-oneself. Sleep-Trust-in-one's-Neighbour.

But what about poetry's heroic qualities, its active life, its civic responsibility?

We must not forget indeed that somewhere at the same time and in the same country Mandelstam – who is needed only by a dozen readers – is actively meeting his death. He has nothing to do with *sleep*. As another poet put it, he knows only a 'great *insomnia*'.

Sleep-Lethe.

Leonid Andreyev describes the risen Lazarus: he has learnt something in Death, he remembers something, something which cannot be defined in human language.

Perhaps he learnt *nothing*?

(How bold we can be in our 'knowledge' of Death).

A friend, regaining consciousness after a deep swoon, says: 'There was nothing, there was not even any 'there', I was, and then. . . – what can I say?. . . – and now – once again – I am'.

There are states of sleep like that swoon.

Sleep which is often, with 'poetic imprecision', compared to death.

When public truth is impossible, the *poet-as-tribune* is replaced by the *platform poet*. The connection between such a poet and the public is like a mutual agreement to 'play at truth' ('we know the truth, – we have left it at home, – that is not why we have gathered here – why talk about unpleasant things, better enjoy ourselves').

What place is there here for *Sleep*, with its anxieties, its complicated, tragic *Individuality* (for a person's *sleep* is perhaps his Individuality – expanded – both self-trusting and searching, confessing, demanding?).

18

And even so, the comparison of Sleep with Death (a very frequent, almost universal one) is conventional and approximate. In such cases, is it not as if we knew something about Death-in-Itself (as if we knew what It contained)? We know Its traces, we know our fear of It. Comparing Sleep with Death, we are most probably speaking only of this fear.

Schopenhauer astonishes me when he gives such a categorical definition of sleep as time 'borrowed from Death'.

19

Who were the poets of whom Mayakovsky exclaimed: 'I'm fed up' at the start of his most active career? Annensky, Tyutchev, Fet. The very poets in whose poetry there is the most *sleep* in all of Russian literature.

There is no *sleep* in Mayakovsky (only dreams, invented, 'constructive'), there is a great deal of it in Pasternak.

20

But at the same time let us give thanks to Sleep (I want to say to Mother-Sleep – it is strange that its gender is masculine in both Russian and French – it must be the God-Sleep), thanks that it is not only a hiding place, a sleeping bag – an imitation of the mother's lap – thanks that the surge of its waves also bakes something for the hearing we know as 'poetic', – 'bakes like waffles'* – remembered in the blood–sound-clusters of darkness, – disposing them – between pauses of emptiness – like shadow-boundaries – of non-paper spaces! – which can, however, also define 'poetic spaces'; thanks – for its light-clusters gleaming, perhaps, like faces – still unknown (oh every night – in sleep – these light-images – with shadow-hieroglyphs!). . .

Indistinct, 'sea-like' labour of sleep! – we believe in it as a lover believes in the life-giving influence of this beloved.

But – 'practically' – how often we turn to Sleep (not intending to, and thus giving ourselves entirely) for 'artistic' help. A life of conscious thought will not take us to those reminiscences, those depths of memory which sleep can display in a moment of illumination. The 'Phonotèque' and 'Phototèque' of the Empire of Sleep are, by the grace of Sleep, always at our disposal, and they

*A quotation from Pasternak's *Second Birth*

contain 'photographs' and 'recordings' of the most complex feelings, the most ancient – and thus the freshest – and most subtle of observations.

Let me repeat here the confession I once made to a friend: 'It may seem funny, but I have to say that I write my best things on the very brink of sleep'.

Of course, this is a special kind of sleep. . .

The poet would gladly agree to things being arranged so that he could do without food. Indeed, it would be better for him. But do not deprive him of *sleep*, Lord. . .

21

'I trust people who get up early', admits a young woman.

There are poets who do not concern themselves with the material of *sleep*. There are those who are often concerned with it, but they are fighters against sleep, *sleepfighters*. René Char. Mandelstam is without doubt an 'early riser'.

22

Sleep-Whisper. Sleep-Roar.

Man is rhythm.

Sleep must in all ways 'permit' this rhythm to be itself (not to be diminished or interrupted by the influence of other rhythms).

Sleep-Poem-in-its-own-right.

23

You could put it this way: a human being is his or her sleep, the character of the sleep contains the character of the person.

Dostoevsky's *sleep*: 'I sleep and wake as many as ten times in one night, every hour or less, often sweating'.

It is like a film which breaks in an almost methodical way when it is projected. Similarly, in Dostoevsky's novels (and particularly their concluding sections) a series of chapters one after another finish with an explosion of events.

As a person takes decisions in relation to life and death, so he manifests his will in relation to *sleep*.

Sleep, which is given us for *rest*, can be transformed into a means of *self-forgetting*.

Sleep-Love-of-self.

To experience oneself. To delight in visions, in *sleep*. For consolation and joy one's own self is enough. A person experiences his own feelings, his flesh, almost his 'own atoms'.

How this resembles the love of intoxication. (In the same way, how a so-called 'drunken delirium' resembles dreams).

A subject for a thesis: 'Sleep in the literature of southern and northern countres'. In which is it more present?

Northern darkness envelops man like the indistinct material of *sleep*.

Sleep exists at both poles of the opposition 'Happiness-Unhappiness'.

Reduce these notions to the antithesis 'Joy-Grief' and sleep disappears.

Sleep likes to inhabit broad notions. We find it in 'war', but not in 'battle'.

'I belong to the gods', said Velemir Khlebnikov in his poem 'For ten years the Russians threw stones at me', a kind of last will and testament.

And his sleep is the sleep of Blessedness. The sleep of the *holy sinner* (undirected blessedness of sleep).

> Sene, son of sky,
> Sow somnolent sable and strength
> On settlement and soil.
> Chary of day, with a chalice
> Of blue wine charm
> Me, earthdweller, with the wave
> Of one foot breaking
> After another.

This is such a 'lyre-like voice' that it seems as if Pushkin would have gasped in quiet rapture at these lines.

Khlebnikov the futurian, unlike the other Russian futurists, belongs to the 'sleepers', the dreamers. But he is vigilant too, like a tempted saint. Later in the same poem we read:

> My steps,
> Mortal steps, are sequence of will.
> My mortal locks I bathe
> In the blue vapour of your quiet
> Waterfall and suddenly shout
> And break spells; the surface formed
> By a straight line which joins
> In 317 days earth and sun
> Is equal to a rectangle's surface
> One side of which is the earth's
> Diameter, the other the road
> Light treads in one year. And you rise
> In my reason, holy figure
> Of 317, among clouds
> Which do not believe.

Will shakes off *Sleep*. And the mathematical calculations of time begin (they take up the second half of the poem, I have cited only a small part of it).

28

Sleep-Light. . .Sleep-Illumination.

Whence this sudden Sea of Light? Perhaps it is a 'cyclical' return of the causeless Unhoped-for Joy?*

Sleep-Healing.

---

*The name of a famous icon, used in Blok's poetry.

29

The dream of Petya Rostov before his death is not just a dream, so powerfully and fundamentally is it directed by the young man's musical gift. Here, at the second level of this dream, we have: Sleep-the-creator, Sleep-the-artist, man-the-artist. Expanded plenitude of the human being (everything in him is 'switched on', the sleep-artist, the sleep-man too has 'begun to speak'). And perhaps – as if something were 'switched off' – the waking-man, who a moment before was busy – with battle (not the fullness of War!) – is really a 'narrow man'.

30

Even if we have got up in good time, and haven't even taken half an hour's sleep at the expense of our nearest and dearest, even so, 'on waking we feel somehow guilty, as if we had behaved badly towards someone', as a friend of mine said recently.

Were we too freely, too 'unreservedly' occupied with ourselves in sleep? Did we allow ourselves 'everything'?

Clearly there is a kind of sleep where conscience does indeed 'doze off'.

31

There is no *sleep* in my *rose-poems*. They are the opposite of *sleep-poems*. Waking, beloved waking (I have written of 'dangerous waking, containing the loved ones') is the incandescence of roses flowering.

32

Look at a person whom not long before you disliked, who perhaps even provoked hostile feelings in you, look at him as he sleeps.

For some reason you will feel pity for him. Pity for his sleeves that stick out, for his hands. . . Pity for his clothes, for some reason. (Awake, his costume resembled 'worldly', 'institutional' even 'family' armour).

He is all trust in Something, in Somebody. And naturally in Someone, who is immeasurably greater than you, the observer.

But even so, there is here also a trust in You.

33

Insomnia. No-Sleep. Antipodes of Sleep, ominous, hostile to us. Sleep's double defined by a 'No'. For it is not just that we 'cannot sleep'. And it is more than Pseudo-Sleep. It is as if for hours on end we are penetrated by disintegration of 'No' atoms. Not death, but a demonstration of destruction, a display of the 'means' by which our gradual, 'natural' end is prepared.

34

Let us imagine now the watchful sleep of a hunted man, who in his sleep expects to be attacked, caught, beaten. His face is like a screen, and he will awake if even a feeble shadow falls on this screen. Transparent, translucent face. And through this partition seems to peer – the soul.

Sleep is the cultivator of our fears. It intensifies them, weakening our resistance to them.

But where do we not see this face-screen, this transparent *partition*?

There is the repulsive sleep (if you have had occasion to see it) of *thugs*. The same sleeves, parts of the body and clothing which in the previous case made you feel pity, do not now seem abandoned to the power of God's will, but remain real, 'belonging to the day', 'ready for living', *looking at you* in the familiar *everyday way*; all this collection of corners of clothing and projections of the body is indeed only *resting*.

Oh, Sleep-Ablution! How can we deserve to be visited by you? Wash away, carry off these images – the raw material of nightmares!

In poems about *insomnia* the word 'conscience' is constantly recurring. No-Sleep (not just the 'absence of sleep') penetrates to the pivot of a man.

And the most '*conscience-bound*' of Russian poets, the

one who more than anyone works with *conscience,* Innokenty Annensky, is the greatest martyr to Insomnia in the whole of world poetry.

His 'Old Estonian Women' is a poem close to shouting about insomnia and it is subtitled 'Fragments of a nightmarish conscience'.

Annensky's *Sleep-poems* are also agonizing; they do not descend into sleep, but leave the sphere of sleep for sorrow, for the cold dawn of searching, tormenting self-consciousness.

39

And now, suddenly waking in the darkness, not yet having had time to get your thoughts together enough to begin again to *love yourself with them,* you will suddenly feel that a certain 'you' is a strange, heterogeneous, and because of the impossibility of experiencing certain emptinesses, a partly-*unlawful* place;

you will suddenly realise that you are not so completely and utterly 'I', self-consciousness, – suddenly, like something empty, you will uncover in yourself – in 'topographically' – undefined gaps – both 'regions' of dust and ashes, and regions of such lifeless 'materiality', such as is built (as if on a building site!), and seems made for spades, for the hammer, for the windy street;

(and now, for some reason you find yourself in a corridor, and what if that is all there is, what if from here you will *never* return *to anything*; – and you will be – unexpectedly – *so abolished*, – nothing but 'not', and soon thought too will be extinguished and only the *corridor* will remain; – and those sleeping beside you? –

who represented to them conversation, presence, exis-
tence, – will remain like that – afterwards – at table –
opening wide – their mouths – with astonishment?. .), –

such, in the intervals of sleep, are you, suddenly find-
ing yourself in a corridor, as if in a remote corner of some
deserted, universal Mistiness.

40

And even so, 'let us plunge into the night'.*
There are people there. There, in the depths of sleep, is
the communion of the living and the dead.

And just as we do not picture the souls of the dead as
'social' or 'national', so, if only in sleep, let us be trustful
in the souls of the living, – and for this let us wish
ourselves clear sleep, *sleep* which seems to have forgiven
us.

For who besides Poetry would allow himself to do
this?. . .

Moscow, 20-24 January 1975

*Quotation from Kafka.

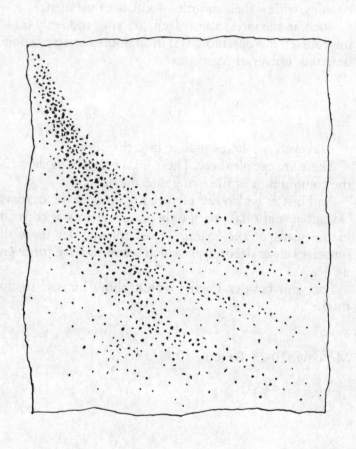